Foreward

Alright, the fact that your reading this right now tells me a lot about you. I am happy that you are here and we're going to discuss a lot in my book, so I want you to pay close attention.

My guess is that you're reading this book and you are new to real estate, which is fine because we all started at this point. My goal is to help you transition from a real estate newbie into a real estate expert in your particular area. I've flipped over 100 plus properties since 2009 as well as helped hundreds of successful students across the country, some even on the other side of the world.

Beyond reading this book and immediately putting these steps into action, I want you to commit to visiting our site: http:// escapethenewbiezone.com to listen to our weekly podcasts.

Every week, I'm giving away tons of content which will help you in your real estate investing business. On Escaping The REI Newbie Zone podcast I interview other real estate experts all around the country. The podcast has been streamed in 50 plus countries and has over 100 plus 5-star ratings on Itunes.

Now, one of the best ways to break into real estate investing is getting started in real estate wholesaling. The reason is because real estate wholesaling is probably the most effective way to bring in tons of money closing deals without you barely having any skin in the game. Basically what I am implying is that this method doesn't require much risk at all. It's little to no risk at all getting started with real estate wholesaling.

Contents

Escaping The REI Newbie Zone Book

By: Chris Bruce

Introduction

Man, I hated working a job. I would go from job to job looking for a new experience and a better way to make more money. I got bored quickly, so after a few months of working somewhere I would quit and find a new job. I had several dead end jobs, but the one I could not stand was being behind a cubicle answering phones. Unfortunately, answering phones was the only job I could qualify for that paid decently.

To be honest, I barely passed high school and didn't even end up graduating on time. I had to attend summer school in order to get my diploma. I tried college but soon realized school was just not for me. I moved from Detroit, MI to Tampa, FL in summer 2004. I remember getting a Temporary job making $12/hr. With tons of overtime available, this money was ok at my age. However, the more money I made the more Uncle Sam would take out of my check.

I ended up stumbling across real estate investing in 2006. This was when the market was red hot. I mean you could literally put a sign in front of a doghouse and it would sell. One day, my dad who lives in Jamaica called me up and told me he had an opportunity for me to make some money. Of course, my eyes lit up and my ears were ready to hear about the opportunity. He said, "Chris I have an opportunity for you to buy a house in Detroit, and make some good money upfront."

I said, "How? Tell me more." I, later on, agreed to buy what would be my first rental property in 2006. Here I was, 22 years old buying a house with a $99k mortgage. I later found out they took money out the equity and gave me $9k to pocket. I'm not even sure if this was all the way legal, but I trusted these people. Fast forward to a year later and I ended up foreclosing on that same property. This was all during the time we all witnessed one of the worst economic crisis ever seen. The recession damaged and crashed the whole housing market. People were hit hard with this crash, including me. By that time I was working for Countrywide Mortgage which was later bought out by Bank of America. The job was fairly easy but after 2 years of working there, I began to get bored. I also had not just me to worry about but also my daughter who was born that February.

I felt like no matter how hard I would try to get ahead I kept drowning in debt and more bills. I remember one day in July after being late on my car note payment for the 3rd time, my car was finally repossessed. That day I had a defining moment, I promised myself from this day on, I'm going to find a way to make money and be able to quit my job (**Just Over Broke**).

So I began to search online, and I came across

WHOLESALING REAL ESTATE ...

Back then I didn't know much about real estate, I only knew the traditional way of buying a home, fixing it up, and then re-selling it to a financed buyer. However after the BOOM (2007-2008) of real estate crashed, I wasn't sure that real estate was a profitable business anymore. There were so many foreclosures taking place and the banks weren't lending out money as easy as they used too.

So being skeptical, I decided to move on to other ventures and put real estate on the back-burner. I tried all types of different Network Marketing pyramid schemes, which I completely sucked at. I later started my 1st business called Luxury Escapes. It was a traveling company, which was supposed to service people on booking their vacations.

Unfortunately, that business never took off and I lost a few hundred bucks that I had invested into it. I even fell victim for a few of those get rich quick scams on making money online. Fool me once, shame on you, fool me twice shame on me.

I was tired of being sick and tired....

I was fed up with failing at every business I tried, so I decided to give this whole Real Estate Wholesaling a try. I said, " What the heck, I've failed at everything else so I might as well give this a try." So after searching for education online about real estate wholesaling, I came across a guy named Preston Ely. He was a seasoned Real Estate Guru, and the funny thing is he was flipping houses right in my neck of the woods in Tampa, FL. What a coincidence, right?

He had a course on how to flip banked own properties called REO Rock Star. I didn't have the cash to purchase the course, so I begged my girlfriend at the time to put it on her credit card. The home study course was $997. After finally being convinced that this was going to lead us to financial freedom, she caved. I was so excited to take on this new journey.

So what exactly is wholesaling? You might ask. Wholesaling is where you agree to purchase a property for a certain price. You place a contract to purchase it and then you turn around and sell your rights to that contract to another buyer for a higher fee. So, for instance, let's say you find a house that's worth $100k. You agree to purchase it for $40k from a homeowner, and then you turn around and sell it for $50k to a cash buyer. You make the middle amount of $10k.

Since it's a cash transaction, you get paid quickly. Everything from the closing transaction is handled by a licensed title company or licensed attorney. It's the simplest way to make money in real estate. The best part is, did you know you don't need cash or credit to purchase the house? You don't even need to be a licensed realtor to do these type of transactions. It's 100% legal in all 50 plus states in the U.S.

One thing I told myself is that this has to work… No excuses. I'm going to go hard on this no matter how long it takes me to be successful. I was very determined and super motivated after going through the home study course.

I began to take action connecting with real estate agents, putting in offers with the banks, looking at houses, etc. Now the only thing I wished I had back then was a mentor. I had always heard it's easier to succeed at something when having access to someone who had already accomplished what you're trying to do. Now at the time, I couldn't afford a real estate mentor. However, looking back I was limiting my thinking.

You don't always need money to get someone to hire you. Look at your skills and what service or value you can provide for someone. If you can exchange value for a little coaching, then you both get something out of the deal. Let's say you're good at building websites or you agree to cold call leads for another investor. This could be your door into getting coaching in exchange to learn from someone who's at the level you desire to be at one day.

Now I wish I could tell you I just got the course and made money the same month. However, that's far from the truth. I actually placed a contract on 26 properties and didn't sell any. I had to back out of all of the contracts and this ruined some of my relationships with agents and other investors. You see, even though I had a real estate course which was a great start I wished I would've had a mentor. This would've saved me all the hassles and mistakes I repeatedly made when first starting out.

Now that I look back on it, I'm glad I went through it. I promised that one day when I became successful, I would try and help as many people as I could to not deal with the same issues I did when I first started.

After what seemed to be the longest few months of my life, I finally landed my 1st real estate deal for $5,000. I made an offer on a property for $30,000 and later found a buyer that wanted to pay me $36,500 on the deal. So after everything was said and done with the transactional funding costs and closing costs, I had a check in my hand for $5,000

Yes! Finally, all the hard work paid off. I was successful, and I began to do this over and over and over again. Now there are a few things I'm going to show you that has helped me since 2009 to be successful and how to duplicate my system. Trust me this is not just a book real estate or about my life. It's more than that my friend. This will be training and you'll walk away with actions steps of what you need to do to get your first real estate deal closed.

You see, I failed all those previous businesses before and I even failed several times in Real Estate. I still fail at my businesses today. However, one thing I didn't do is give up and I grew my mindset to be able to handle every objection or problem that came my way. Think about Michael Jordan no matter how many shots he would miss he would continue taking them because he knew the next time he would make it. He might miss 4 in a row, but that never stopped him from shooting again and again. Now Michael Jordan is arguably one of the best players ever to touch a basketball.

It's the same mindset you have to adapt if you want to be a successful real estate wholesaler. Your business and bank account will only grow to the extent that you do.

After reading the book <u>Secrets Of The Millionaire Mind</u>, I realized what's keeping me broke is not lack of ability. It's not the lack of opportunity. It's not lack of luck.

It's lack of Knowledge

"The Rich guy isn't any better than you. He simply knows things that you don't."

-T Harv Eker – Secrets Of The Millionaire Mind

Make sure you read that book twice. The first time I picked up that book I couldn't put it down. I ended up finishing it in Barnes and Nobles in just 48 hours. I put a bookmark in the book and went back the next day to finish it. I later purchased the book. You will be amazed that the financial state you're in right now has nothing to do with why you think you're stuck there. Unless you're reading this and you're already rich.

I have a few more books I want to recommend you read. I know you're ready for me to get into the "how to" of real estate and I will soon. Understand your mind must arrive at your destination before you do. That's why I read 3- 5 books a month. Now I know you might be saying, "well that's easy for you Chris since you're a full-time entrepreneur." However, when I started off part-time wholesaling while still working a full-time job, I would at least read a chapter a day.

This helped build up my mindset and confidence while going through the daily grind. Most people never achieve their dreams not because they didn't have the skills, but they didn't have the right mindset. It's not easy running a business, if someone tells you it is they are lying. It becomes simple however when you follow the blueprint of successful people before you.

Books To Read:

Rich Dad Poor Dad - Robert Kiyosaki

Be You Be Great - Antonio Edwards

The Four Hour Workweek - Tim Ferris

The Abundance Loop - Julianna Park

How To Get Out Your Own Way - Tyrese Gibson

Change Your Brain Change Your Life - Daniel Amen MD

Emerging Real Estate Markets - David Lindahl

The 5 Things Not To Do: When First Starting

Alright, so 1 thing you don't want to do is a mistake that I made, which is to become a landlord first. Yes, the key to having freedom is through creating residual income and building up your assets, but you never want to start off trying to build up your asset column. For instance, like becoming a landlord without having some extra reserves set aside.

I tell anybody that wants to be a landlord to at least have $50,000 - 100,000 dollars in your bank account before you become a landlord. This nest egg is basically to ensure if anything was to happen with the property that you're maintaining that you have enough money to cover expenses or any type of repairs needed for the tenant living in your property.

Okay, rule number two. Do not waste every single dollar you have buying every single real estate course out there. The reason why I say this is because a lot of people especially the ones starting off new into real estate get caught up with the shiny objects and wanting to buy every single product. Now there's nothing wrong with educating yourself and I do highly suggest you pick 1 or 2 of the products out there. This does not mean buy a new product every single month folks, lol.

Because what will happen is you will get information overload and trying to process all of the information from the real estate courses will drive you crazy.

Rule number three, do not try to learn everything in real estate investing before you get started in actually taking action. The real estate investing game is about taking action and if you want to learn every single thing before you get started you will throw away so much time that you could be going out there closing real estate deals and making money.

Some people end up looking at wholesaling real estate like college, where you have to actually educate yourself for many years and then you can actually go into your profession. As if this won't work unless you've started making money, well I am here to tell you that is simply not the case in real estate wholesaling.

In fact, I've had 1 of my students who recently got started and less than 45 days he closed his first real estate deal for $9k and didn't know what the heck he was doing. Not to mention he lived in a whole different country. It's what we call Virtual Wholesaling, but I'll explain more on that later.

There are so many components to real estate investing that it will pretty much be impossible to learn everything before you get started. So the main thing is to educate yourself on one topic and then start to get out there, take massive action, and you will start to see results.

There is a famous quote, I always like to tell people this 1 thing, you don't have to be great to start, but you have to start to be great!

"You may delay, but time will not." — **Benjamin Franklin**

Alright, rule number 4, do not forget one of the most important things that you should be doing when you're starting off in real estate wholesaling, and that is **marketing**. Marketing is the key and lifeline of your real estate business. I tell people all the time when it comes to wholesaling you're in the marketing and people business. You have to market to find deals and buyers if you want to get paid.

If you don't continue to market you will not bring in leads, and you will not be able to make offers on deals, which means no deals under contract, you get the point… Okay, so marketing is the key thing that you must do in your business each and every single day.

I've talked with a lot of real estates newbie's, and the 1 thing that they always complain about is not having enough deals, and when I sit down and ask them what type of marketing they are doing? Typically, they don't have much to say. Think of it like watching TV and you keep seeing that same cheeseburger on the McDonald's commercial pop up. Now me personally I don't like McDonald's but hey, to each is own.

See when you see that new Big Mac cheeseburger that they are advertising, they continue to market it to you on commercial after commercial after commercial. It's being marketed in a certain way to you that it looks so delicious and you have to go and get it. It's the same thing with your real estate business the only difference is that you're marketing your service and business to people instead of an actual product.

Last but not least, do not forget that when it comes to real estate wholesaling it's not so much about buying and selling properties. You have to focus on being in the people business and not forgetting about servicing the customer.

Yes, our main goal is to buy and sell the house and pick up that big check. In order for that to happen, we provide a service to homeowners who are in need of selling their home. Let's say for instance someone who just inherited a home after their mom passed. They live in California and have a house in Ohio. He or she is not willing to be a landlord and rent the place out. In fact, he/she doesn't want anything to do with the house they rather sell it for quick cash.

That's when you come into the picture and provide a quick cash closing to the seller. They walk away with cash and relief because they no longer have to deal with a property out of state. Your buyer walks away with a new house with tons of equity. You walk away with a new fat check in your bank account. A win-win solution for everyone.

There are tons of situations why someone would need to sell their home. It's your responsibility to dig deeper, maybe the seller recently lost a job or is going through a divorce. Maybe they're tired of getting burnt by the tenants or tired of being a landlord and always having to evict tenants.

Whatever the case is, our main goal is to find whatever the problem that they're having and be the solver of that problem. People do business with people that they like and trust so you must quickly engage, build rapport, and get the trust of that seller so that they will sign the paperwork allowing you to purchase their home. It's like being a real estate therapist. You'll actually enjoy your business, and you'll make a lot of money doing it.

Now you might be wondering well just how much money can you make in this new venture? It all depends on a few variables. I've made upwards of $32,000 on one single deal. Most of my wholesale deals in my market of Tampa, FL average around $6,000 - $10,00. I've had students who've done deals and made $50,000 on one single deal. I saw in a real estate forum a deal where a guy made $100,000.

The amount you can earn is limitless. It's all about how low you agree to purchase the property. You make money by buying low and selling high. One way to ensure how much you can make on a single deal is by running comparables on the property. Finding out not just how much the house is worth, but also how much properties are selling for in that area that compares to your subject property.

After you find out the MAO, your maximum allowable offer, then you'll know what to offer the seller. Let's say the comparables come back on a house I have for $50- $52k. If I go to the seller and offer $40k, then it's a good chance I'll make close to $10k selling that deal.

How Do I Get Started?

Alright, first things in wholesaling you have to understand! You're in the business to find A=Motivated Seller contract (The property), you are B=Wholesaler, who will then sell your contract, to C=End Buyer. Which is typical a rehabber that will fix it and re-sell or a Landlord who will rent it out for Cash flow? But even before you go out to find motivated sellers you need to understand your market.

You can do this by doing your market research. Now there are a few ways you can do this. I'll explain the most common ones I use and teach all my students to do.

I like to partner up with a realtor and start to build a relationship with them. Let them know I'm an investor, and I'm looking to work closely with a top agent like them to buy properties in the area. I also let them know the benefit they will receive by working with me. I'm doing this because in exchange I'll be asking for them to send me a list of the recent 90-day cash transactions in the area.

In fact, I have a script I provide to all my students which I'll share with you here below in Exhibit A:

Exhibit A:

You: Hi, My name is (insert name here) I'm a real estate investor new to the area, but not new to investing. I'm looking to start buying some properties, and I'm looking to work with top-notch agents/realtors like yourself to take some of those listings off your hand and make you a lot of money. I also get properties from homeowners that are just priced too high for me to buy. Frankly, since I can't do anything with them, instead of throwing the leads away, I rather just give them all to you for you to list and make money on them.

Since I'm new to this area and want to get started making offers with you, I need to know the hottest areas where everyone's buying and selling. Can you send me a list of the past cash sales in the area within the past 90 days? I'd appreciate it. (Listen to what the realtor says. Let him/her know he can just email it to you)

Now, this script has been tried and test in over 35 different markets and has worked time after time. Remember you must lead with value and always give the other person what's in it for them first. Too many people get this wrong, don't be one of them.

Now let's say you can't get in touch with any realtors or you're having trouble finding one that will work with you. Fine, like I mentioned, there are other ways you can go about by finding the hot areas in your market. Another good strategy is by using a website service that sells lists like listsouce.com or melissadata.com. Both sites sell absentee owner lists. Now you might have to purchase the list in order to view it, but it's like eight cents a lead, so it's very inexpensive.

You can use this to look up absentee owners in your county, or city and state. Search for properties where the last sales date was 90 days prior to the current date. Pay attention to those zip codes and start to write down the hot ones that you see keep coming up. Then, purchase a map and start to map out where those areas are in your city. This is where you'll want to start dumping your marketing.

The common mistake I see people do is marketing for houses all over their town. Some of those areas are not even desirable for investors. Then they wonder why they can't sell the house. Do your market research first!

Moving along… Marketing and how to get started

Network

I can't tell you how many times students of mine have made money with me, and when I ask where their leads are coming from they reply, "*just getting out there and talking to people.*" And they're telling the God's honest truth. I started out by getting business cards printed up. My cards said "I buy houses any situation, any condition" with my email address and phone number.

I set a goal of how many I would pass out per day and stuck to it. If you don't like talking to strangers, you are going to need to overcome this. Simply force yourself to do it (keeping your goal of reaching a better financial status clearly in mind for motivational support) and then your feelings will quickly change.

Flyers

You can print unlimited flyers from the comfort of your home computer for merely the price of paper. Simply run your behind up and down streets, sticking them on the outsides of mailboxes until you're rich and skinny.

Free Online Classified Ads

This is by far my favorite free thing to do. For obvious reasons (No manual labor). I recommend Craigslist and Backpage. I'm sure there are others. Write in and tell me about them if you have any success. You can post ads there for free, and you WILL get leads. An added bonus is the search engines often times pick these ads up and display them for the world to see, for FREE. Get out there and make it happen, my friend.

Hire Bird Dogs

Almost every investor I know uses bird dogs a.k.a lead finders to help bring them find deals. The good thing is you can advertise for people to be your bird dog and bring you leads. I have a great system I use to hire, track, and manage my bird dogs. The good thing is that I don't pay them for their services until the deals close. I have actively 30 bird dogs to this day that bring leads to me in every county I invest in. Now you can't legally use the term bird dog.

I tend to say Motivated Lead Finder.

If you want it - you'll get it.

Now I can't stand foreclosures!

This is simply because I don't like stress. Some stress is good. However, the stress of losing your home is no Bueno (been taking Spanish lessons, forgive me.)

The fact of the matter, there's a lot of people all across the country in foreclosure, or about to go into foreclosure. I'm averse to doing foreclosures simply because to me it seems like a big hassle. With that being said, tracking down the sellers who are hiding out in a closet with a shotgun and a canteen, stopping auctions, and dealing with banks are the ones seeking help.

In that case, if you find those people you should do foreclosures. So do as I say, and not as I do. Seriously, you can literally go into any public place right now, and I bet you will pass several people that are in foreclosure right now. Everyone is in foreclosure right now. This world is crawling with paranoid, delusional, motivated sellers with shotguns and canteens. So here are 3 keys to hunting down these owners of pre-foreclosures

Key #1 - Get a List of All the Properties in Foreclosure

My suggestion is to go down to your county courthouse and get this information for free. After doing this for some time, you will probably run into someone there who actually goes every day and sells the lists so that you don't have to do it anymore.

Key #2 - Find the Seller

This is what separates the pros from the not-so-pros. You can look up the owner of the record via public records. Then head over to www.findtheseller.com or www.Microbilt.com. This is skip-tracing software. Put in the seller's name, narrow the search down by the state, and then the city and then it will spit out the seller's 10 digits. It spits him right out of the computer screen. It's very convenient and scary at the same time. Just think anyone can find your phone number on this website. You might want to look yourself up there.

Key #3 – Mail out Yellow Letters or Postcards

Make these very basic. Your main point in doing this is to find out which one's come back undeliverable. These are your hot leads.

Tip of the day: Vacant house + owner in pre-foreclosure = Hot Lead

P.S.: If you would like for me to hold your hand & walk you through your 1st Real Estate Deal.

Create your own personal action plan as you go through the experience. Certain things will resonate with you personally. You will want to implement these things immediately.

Now there are many other lists I target besides pre-foreclosures. These lists are high equity & free and clear owners, probates, as well as tax defaults. Marketing to these leads has always generated me the most leads and revenue in terms of wholesaling. So let me take the time to break down each lead source. Beginning with high equity and free and clear seller leads.

High Equity & Free & Clear

Targeting off-market properties, our go-to list has always been high equity, free and clear leads. What this means is that the homeowner either has a very small mortgage left or the house is paid off. I typically target homeowners that also have been living in their house for at least 10 years or longer and are over the age of 55. There are several list brokers that sell these types of lists including Melissa Data and List Source. We even take it as far as scrubbing that list again to find which one of those houses are vacant and target them specifically.

I typically mail them out a postcard showing interest that I'm looking to purchase a property like theirs. If you would like to get a copy of that postcard text the word TEMPLATES to the number 33444. Just reply back with your email address, and I'll send it to you for free.

Now when it comes to mailing postcards, I use a website called click2mail.com. It's very inexpensive to send out postcards, and you can upload your lists and create your postcards all online. You can even train a Virtual Assistant or outsource this task to someone else. The good thing with this service is unlike other companies they don't require you to have a huge budget.

Now if you are looking into mailing bulk like 3000 plus at a time, I highly recommend you use a service like Go Big Printing. I've used them in the past, just make sure you have the manpower and staff to handle all the calls coming in. I highly recommend you set up a separate phone number to handle the call flow.

I use Freedomsoft to capture and handle my calls now, but in the past I've used google voice. The great thing about google voice is it is 100% free.

Probates & Tax Defaults

These two leads sources are probably the most profitable homeowners you need to be targeting. I absolutely love probate deals, and I've found that in some markets investors aren't even targeting this lead source at all. Countless times I've had heirs from the personal estate call me and thank me that I sent them a letter. They also mentioned that I was the only one who mailed a letter to them expressing interest in buying their home.

Just in case you don't know what probates are they are when someone dies and their will is not filled out correctly. The house then goes through a legal process (probate) to establish who gets what. In many cases, there are homes left in the estate. These heirs that inherit the property 9 out of 10 times don't typically want to keep the property. They would rather sell it for quick cash. Also, there isn't a lot of emotional attachment to the property. They didn't spend hours cutting the grass, making sure the house renovations and updates were done, or spend a lifetime trying to pay the mortgage.

It's very common to get these deals way under market value. When it comes to wholesaling, that's music to my ears.

Now with tax defaults, these people are getting ready to lose their home if they don't pay their taxes off. When you buy a home, you're not only responsible for paying your mortgage but also your yearly taxes. That's not a problem because the banks will wrap that into your monthly mortgage cost. However once it's paid off, some homeowners have a hard time keeping up with that lump sum payment a year.

Many of these homeowners have not paid taxes on their homes in years. So Uncle Sam will be looking to collect, or they will lose their home. You can access these leads from your local courthouse.

Negotiating & Getting Your Offers Accepted

When first starting out, negotiating with sellers is always that thing you dread doing. I mean you're nervous hoping the seller will accept your offer. My mentor always told me if you're not afraid of your offer then you're offering to high. So how can you get more offers accepted? What things should you say or not say?

I can say your chances of getting your offer accepted will be much higher when dealing with a truly motivated seller. Like I said before, there is a big difference from someone who's been thinking about selling and decides heck let me see what I can get for the property versus someone who has a dire need to sell their property due to specific situation especially if the house is in need of renovations or updates. This will work very good in your favor. So the first thing you should do is find out what's the reason for them wanting to sell their property. One question you can ask is, "Which would you say is more important selling the property quickly or holding out for the best price?" This will let you know if they're motivated to sell. Always let them know that you won't be able to pay retail for the property.

Another thing you want to let the sellers know is all of the benefits you provide. You don't charge commissions since you're not a realtor. Even if you are in this process you won't be acting as a realtor; you're the investor. You pay all closing costs and will buy the house with cash, AS IS. Always try and get the seller to give you a ballpark price of what they would like to get for the property.

Major key - Always negotiate in front of something that needs to be repaired. So for instance, if the bathroom is outdated, or the flooring needs to be replaced, you'll want to give your offer and discuss price at that time. It's easier to remind them that you'll be doing them a huge favor not having to fix that broken toilet and tiling.

Now before negotiating the deal, you'll want to have run comparables (comps for short) prior. You'll want to know the ARV after repair value, and even more importantly the MAO maximum allowable offer. To find the ARV, you'll want to search sites like Zillow or Redfin. Type in the property address and start to look at what other houses in the area sold for recently. You can add the price of the 3 nearest houses that sold and then divide that by 3 to get the ARV. This will give you an average of what properties are selling for in that area.

Rule of thumb, always compares oranges to oranges. So make sure to compare 2 bedrooms 1 bathroom houses with other 2 bedrooms 1 bathroom houses that are within a mile and a half radius. Try and compare how close the house was built to the subject property as possible. Also don't forget about the square feet as well. You don't want to compare a house 3,000 sq ft to a house that's only 980 sq ft.

When it comes to finding the MAO, it's all about finding what prices of homes sold for cash. Like the ARV, you want to find similar houses that have sold, but you want to filter out the financed sold homes. Since you'll be buying with cash, you want to find houses most comparable to yours that sold for $50k cash. It's easier to formulate what you'll be offering the seller.

Typically I like to offer around $15k less than what other houses sold for. Now there are times when I offer higher. Like for instance if the house is in really good condition. However, I like to give myself a cushion because I like to make at least $10k per deal and leave room for my buyers to make money as well.

Remember you have to buy low and sell low. It has to be a win-win for you and your buyer as well. I use the MLS to provide me with comps and my MAO, so I know what to offer. Now you have to be a licensed realtor to get MLS access. If you get in good with a realtor, you can get them to send you cash comps of the property. What I tell everyone to do is make sure to provide some type of value to the realtor.

You can do this by giving them free listings. Just think about it, you're going to be talking to hundreds of people interested in selling their home. Not all of them will want to sell it at a discount. It's a numbers game when it comes to wholesaling. For those that don't, you can easily refer them to your realtor. You get comps for free, and they get leads for free. BOOM!

Now, once you get your offer accepted, you'll want to get a contract signed by the seller. If you would like to get access to my real estate contract I use, you can go to www.escapethenewbiezone.com. Make sure to take pictures of the property and record a video walkthrough if possible. You'll use this to send to potential cash buyers.

You'll want to let the seller know that you'll still need to get your funding partner in to take a look at it. I always use the term Funding Partner (aka your cash buyer), so it doesn't scare off your seller. If you can get the seller to agree to make a copy of the key, and put a lockbox on the property, then do it. One thing you don't want to do is have a bunch of buyers going to the property scaring the seller off and asking a bunch of questions.

So the next section I'll talk about finding buyers and the process I use to get cash buyers in and out the properties. Also the closing process and how to pick up your first wholesale check!

The fun begins!

The Closing Process: Finding Cash Buyers & Closing the Deal

Now that you have a new deal under contract it's time to find a buyer. Typically you're going to be selling to an investor who will either be a landlord or rehabber. If the house is in an area where it's more rentals, ideally you'll be selling to a landlord. If the area is more of middle-lower high-class area, you'll more likely be selling to a rehabber.

Finding landlord buyers is pretty simple. You can post ads on Craigslist with the headline "Landlords Dream." Post the pictures of the property with your asking price and include beds and baths with sq ft, and have them contact you for more details. I typically won't put the full address, just the street name city and state. This sparks interest and will get the person viewing the ad to call you.

You can also put up bandit signs advertising you have a house for sale. This works really good to attract new buyers. Put about 15-25 of them out after 5 pm on a Friday night. You can get signs from your local handyman shop or Home Depot or Lowes. Make sure the signs are 18 X 24 corrugated signs. Take a friend with you to help you put them out.

Another great way to find cash buyers is by going to your local REIA meetings. There will be other wholesalers there, but also I always find a handful of cash buyers that will show up looking for deals. One of my favorite places to find buyers is auctions. If you've never experienced a live auction, you have to attend at least one. It's fun to watch people fight over deals. You'll gain a few dozen cash buyers by showing up with your deals.

Last but not least, you can contact previous cash buyers that recently bought in the past 90-180 days. The cash buyers that have previously bought will typically buy again, especially when you have a hot deal for them. You can get this type of list from several sources. Mail them a postcard or letter that you have another hot property in the area where they recently bought. Also, include your email and phone number so they can contact you.

Now if you and the seller agreed to put a lockbox on the property, then you can just give buyers the code. Have them look at it and contact you back if they're interested in purchasing it. If you don't have a lockbox on it then you will have to schedule a time for the buyer to go in to see it. Make them do a ride by the property to take a look.

Let the buyer know after seeing the pictures you sent them, and doing the ride by, if they are still interested you'll then schedule a time for them to take a look at it. To not cause any confusion, I let the buyer know up front it's a wholesale deal and not to mention price or anything in front of the seller. I advise the buyer that the seller thinks that they are one of my partners.

After the buyer agrees, they want to move forward with the purchase of the property. Make the buyer sign a purchase contract and hand you a nonrefundable deposit of $2k - $5k. Now don't go spending that deposit money just yet. Take that contract and deposit to a licensed title company or licensed closing attorney. Also, include your contract with the seller.

Now the Title Company or attorney will handle the rest. They'll run the title to make sure it's clean, and send you the HUD. They'll set up the closing. The seller will go and sign their part and pick up their check. Your buyer will go with the rest of the money and pick up their keys. You'll be able to go in and sign your part and pick up your check, or you can have them wire your funds straight to your account.

SUCCESS QUOTE

"Rather than wishing for change, you first must be prepared to change."! ! !

- Catherine Pulsifer

Take action RIGHT THE HECK NOW. Do something. Anything. Order your business cards, bandit signs … whatever. Get the motors going. Don't delay even for a second. Immediate action is required. If you take action now on the things you've learned from this book, you'll have a check in no time.

Sit down and write your goals for creating wealth and profiting In Real Estate today! After you've done that, double them all. Read them out loud every single day until they are a reality. Remember marketing and making offers is the one thing you'll need to be doing daily.

Also, create a list of affirmations based on your goals and say them out loud every day. Don't miss a day. I haven't missed a day in 2 years. You either want it or you don't, my friend.

Firing My Boss & Quitting the Rat Race

So I seem to get this question asked a lot lately. "When is the best time to quit my job, and go full time as an investor?" Well, let me shed some light on this. I'm going to tell you the right and smart thing to do, and what I did.

The Timing Is Never Right.

I remember my friend asked me how I decided when to quit my job. The answer was simple: "It was something I wanted, and I decided there was no point in putting it off. The timing is never right to quit your job." And so it is.

What I suggest is that you build up your bank account. Work hard stacking up at least one year's worth of what you make at your job. This will provide the security if some deals were to fall apart you can still support yourself and keep moving forward. Now if you look at it you're only making $30k a year. This can be achievable by closing 6 deals at $5k a pop.

Of course, you won't know exactly the amount you will make on every deal. Some might be more than $5k while a few might be under. But the average deal in my area is $7k and higher. So again, this isn't a very far-fetched goal. You can close 6 deals in less than 12 months. Heck, you can close 6 deals in less than 2 months, you just have to work hard to get there.

But maybe you're like me. Working a job is standing in the way of you being able to achieve your goals as a real estate investor. Waiting for a good time to quit your job? The stars will never align, and the traffic lights of life will never all be green at the same time. The universe doesn't conspire against you, but it doesn't go out of its way to line up all the pins either. So if it's really important to you and you want to do it "eventually," just do it and correct the course along the way.

Now, one of the most overlooked things in Real Estate and in life is to become rich and wealthy. You have to work hard on growing yourself. It's not all about money. When you grow as a person everything else falls right into place. Ask me how I know? I seriously went from doing no deals to deals falling into my lap once I changed my mindset. I still to this day say affirmations every morning and commit to reading 2-3 books a month.

The key will be to give as much as you can so you can receive as well. The reason why a lot of people don't see a lot of success is because they don't go into their business with the same thought in mind. They're always concerned about how much money they're getting paid before they even brought value to the customer. That is why it's really important to be doing what you are passionate about. When you are passionate about something, you do it better than the average person.

After having a lot of success in Real Estate you can even begin to give back by coaching others. You should always have one hand up to a mentor and one hand down to a mentee. You can begin to create products that will help new struggling investors. This will be your good deed, and maybe even your lifetime goal. The goal in life is to pursue and do whatever it is you were put on this earth to do. If you're not doing that, then you're just going through the motions of life.

To continue your education and get my free course head over to
www.escapethenewbiezone.com

I hope you enjoyed reading this book. The ball is now in your
court. We have several testimonials of 100's of people just like you
who have taken one of our courses or programs and have achieved
a lot of success. Go out and create the financial freedom for
yourself and your family.

I wish you Much Success in your Life Journey!

Don't Live To Dream Live Your Dream - Chris Bruce

Resources:

Official Websites:

www.escapethenewbiezone.com Podcast Blog

YouTube:

www.youtube.com/ChrisBruce

Facebook:

www.facebook.com/DetroitMogul

Instagram:

www.instagram.com/DetroitMogul

Made in the USA
Lexington, KY
25 October 2019